In Celebration of

Date

Guest Name
(address/phone #/email)

Notes

_____

_____

_____

_____

_____

_____

_____

_____

_____

_____

_____

_____

_____

_____

Guest Name
(address/phone #/email)

Notes

Guest Name
(address/phone #/email)

Notes

_____

_____

_____

_____

_____

_____

_____

_____

_____

_____

_____

_____

_____

_____

_____

_____

Guest Name
(address/phone #/email)

Notes

_____

_____

_____

_____

_____

_____

_____

_____

_____

_____

_____

_____

Guest Name
(address/phone #/email)

Notes

Guest Name
(address/phone #/email)

Notes

Guest Name
(address/phone #/email)

Notes

_____

_____

_____

_____

_____

_____

_____

_____

_____

_____

_____

_____

Guest Name
(address/phone #/email)

Notes

Guest Name
(address/phone #/email)

Notes

_____

_____

_____

_____

_____

_____

_____

_____

_____

_____

_____

_____

_____

Guest Name

(address/phone #/email)

Notes

Guest Name
(address/phone #/email)

Notes

_____

_____

_____

_____

_____

_____

_____

_____

_____

_____

_____

_____

_____

Guest Name
(address/phone #/email)

Notes

Guest Name
(address/phone #/email)

Notes

_____

_____

_____

_____

_____

_____

_____

_____

_____

_____

_____

_____

_____

_____

Guest Name
(address/phone #/email)

Notes

_____

_____

_____

_____

_____

_____

_____

_____

_____

_____

_____

_____

_____

_____

_____

_____

_____

Guest Name
(address/phone #/email)

Notes

_____

_____

_____

_____

_____

_____

_____

_____

_____

_____

_____

_____

_____

Guest Name
(address/phone #/email)

Notes

Guest Name
(address/phone #/email)

Notes

_____

_____

_____

_____

_____

_____

_____

_____

_____

_____

_____

_____

_____

_____

_____

Guest Name
(address/phone #/email)

Notes

Guest Name
(address/phone #/email)

Notes

_____

_____

_____

_____

_____

_____

_____

_____

_____

_____

_____

_____

_____

Guest Name
(address/phone #/email)

Notes

Guest Name
(address/phone #/email)

Notes

_____

_____   _____

_____

_____   _____

_____

_____   _____

_____

_____   _____

_____

Guest Name
(address/phone #/email)

Notes

_____

_____

_____

_____

Guest Name
(address/phone #/email)

Notes

_____

_____

_____

_____

_____

_____

_____

_____

_____

_____

_____

_____

_____

Guest Name
(address/phone #/email)

Notes

Guest Name
(address/phone #/email)

Notes

_____

_____

_____

_____

_____

_____

_____

_____

_____

_____

_____

_____

_____

Guest Name
(address/phone #/email)

Notes

Guest Name
(address/phone #/email)

Notes

Guest Name
(address/phone #/email)

Notes

_____

_____

_____

_____

_____

_____

_____

_____

_____

_____

_____

_____

_____

Guest Name
(address/phone #/email)

Notes

_____

_____   _____

_____   _____

_____   _____

                                                     _____

                                                     _____

                                                     _____

                                                     _____

                                                     _____

                                                     _____

                                                     _____

Guest Name
(address/phone #/email)

Notes

_____

_____

_____

_____

_____

_____

_____

_____

_____

_____

_____

_____

_____

_____

_____

Guest Name
(address/phone #/email)

Notes

Guest Name
(address/phone #/email)

Notes

_____

_____

_____

_____

_____

_____

_____

_____

_____

_____

_____

_____

_____

_____

_____

_____

Guest Name
(address/phone #/email)

Notes

_____

_____

_____

_____

_____

_____

_____

_____

_____

_____

_____

_____

_____

_____

Guest Name
(address/phone #/email)

Notes

Guest Name
(address/phone #/email)

Notes

Guest Name
(address/phone #/email)

Notes

Guest Name
(address/phone #/email)

Notes

_____

_____

_____

_____

_____

_____

_____

_____

_____

_____

_____

_____

_____

Guest Name
(address/phone #/email)

Notes

_____

_____

_____

_____

_____

_____

_____

_____

_____

_____

_____

_____

_____

_____

_____

Guest Name
(address/phone #/email)

Notes

_____

_____

_____

_____

_____

_____

_____

_____

_____

_____

_____

_____

_____

Guest Name
(address/phone #/email)

Notes

Guest Name
(address/phone #/email)

Notes

Guest Name
(address/phone #/email)

Notes

Guest Name
(address/phone #/email)

Notes

Guest Name
(address/phone #/email)

Notes

Guest Name
(address/phone #/email)

Notes

Guest Name
(address/phone #/email)

Notes

_____

_____

_____

_____

Guest Name
(address/phone #/email)

Notes

_____

_____

_____

_____

_____

_____

_____

_____

_____

_____

_____

_____

_____

_____

Guest Name
(address/phone #/email)

Notes

Guest Name
(address/phone #/email)

Notes

Guest Name
(address/phone #/email)

Notes

Guest Name
(address/phone #/email)

Notes

_____

_____

_____

_____

Guest Name
(address/phone #/email)

Notes

Guest Name
(address/phone #/email)

Notes

Guest Name
(address/phone #/email)

Notes

Guest Name
(address/phone #/email)

Notes

_____

_____

_____

_____

_____

_____

_____

_____

_____

_____

_____

_____

_____

_____

Guest Name
(address/phone #/email)

Notes

_____

_____

_____

_____

_____

_____

_____

_____

_____

_____

_____

_____

_____

_____

_____

Guest Name
(address/phone #/email)

Notes

_____

_____

_____

_____

_____

_____

_____

_____

_____

_____

_____

_____

_____

_____

Guest Name
(address/phone #/email)

Notes

Guest Name
(address/phone #/email)

Notes

_____

_____

_____

_____

_____

_____

_____

_____

_____

_____

_____

_____

_____

Guest Name
(address/phone #/email)

Notes

Guest Name
(address/phone #/email)

Notes

_____

_____

_____

_____

_____

_____

_____

_____

_____

_____

_____

_____

_____

_____

Guest Name
(address/phone #/email)

Notes

_____

_____

_____

_____

_____

_____

_____

_____

_____

_____

_____

_____

Guest Name
(address/phone #/email)

Notes

_____

_____

_____

_____

Guest Name
(address/phone #/email)

Notes

_____

_____

_____

_____

_____

_____

_____

_____

_____

_____

_____

_____

_____

_____

_____

_____

Guest Name
(address/phone #/email)

Notes

_____

_____

_____

_____

Guest Name
(address/phone #/email)

Notes

_____

_____

_____

_____

_____

_____

_____

_____

_____

_____

_____

_____

_____

_____

_____

_____

Guest Name
(address/phone #/email)

Notes

_____

_____

_____

_____

_____

_____

_____

_____

_____

_____

_____

_____

_____

Guest Name
(address/phone #/email)

Notes

Guest Name
(address/phone #/email)

Notes

_____

_____

_____

_____

_____

_____

_____

_____

_____

_____

_____

_____

_____

Guest Name
(address/phone #/email)

Notes

Guest Name
(address/phone #/email)

Notes

_____

_____

_____

_____

_____

_____

_____

_____

_____

_____

_____

_____

_____

_____

Guest Name
(address/phone #/email)

Notes

_____

_____

_____

_____

_____

_____

_____

_____

_____

_____

_____

_____

_____

_____

Guest Name
(address/phone #/email)

Notes

_____

_____

_____

_____

_____

_____

_____

_____

_____

_____

_____

_____

_____

Guest Name
(address/phone #/email)

Notes

Guest Name
(address/phone #/email)

Notes

_____

_____

_____

_____

_____

_____

_____

_____

_____

_____

_____

_____

_____

_____

Guest Name
(address/phone #/email)

Notes

Guest Name
(address/phone #/email)

Notes

_____

_____

_____

_____

Guest Name
(address/phone #/email)

Notes

Guest Name
(address/phone #/email)

Notes

Guest Name

(address/phone #/email)

Notes

Guest Name
(address/phone #/email)

Notes

_____

_____

_____

_____

_____

_____

_____

_____

_____

_____

_____

_____

_____

_____

_____

_____

Guest Name
(address/phone #/email)

Notes

_____

_____

_____

_____

_____

_____

_____

_____

_____

_____

_____

_____

_____

_____

_____

Guest Name
(address/phone #/email)

Notes

_____

_____

_____

_____

_____

_____

_____

_____

_____

_____

_____

_____

_____

Guest Name
(address/phone #/email)

Notes

_____

_____

_____

_____

_____

_____

_____

_____

_____

_____

_____

_____

_____

Guest Name
(address/phone #/email)

Notes

_____

_____

_____

_____

_____

_____

_____

_____

_____

_____

_____

_____

_____

_____

Guest Name
(address/phone #/email)

Notes

Guest Name
(address/phone #/email)

Notes

_____

_____

_____

_____

Guest Name
(address/phone #/email)

Notes

Guest Name
(address/phone #/email)

Notes

_____

_____

_____

_____

_____

_____

_____

_____

_____

_____

_____

_____

_____

_____

Guest Name
(address/phone #/email)

Notes

_____

_____

_____

_____

_____

_____

_____

_____

_____

_____

_____

_____

_____

_____

Guest Name
(address/phone #/email)

Notes

_____

_____

_____

_____

_____

_____

_____

_____

_____

_____

_____

_____

_____

_____

Guest Name
(address/phone #/email)

Notes

_____

_____

_____

_____

_____
_____
_____
_____
_____
_____
_____
_____
_____
_____
_____

Guest Name
(address/phone #/email)

Notes

_____

_____

_____

_____

_____

_____

_____

_____

_____

_____

_____

_____

_____

_____

Guest Name
(address/phone #/email)

Notes

Guest Name
(address/phone #/email)

Notes

_____

_____

_____

_____

_____

_____

_____

_____

_____

_____

_____

_____

_____

_____

Guest Name
(address/phone #/email)

Notes

Guest Name
(address/phone #/email)

Notes

_____

_____

_____

_____

_____

_____

_____

_____

_____

_____

_____

_____

Guest Name
(address/phone #/email)

Notes

_____

_____

_____

_____

Guest Name
(address/phone #/email)

Notes

_____

_____

_____

_____

Guest Name
(address/phone #/email)

Notes

Guest Name
(address/phone #/email)

Notes

_____

_____

_____

_____

Guest Name
(address/phone #/email)

Notes

_____

_____

_____

_____

_____

_____

_____

_____

_____

_____

_____

_____

_____

_____

_____

Guest Name
(address/phone #/email)

Notes

_____

_____

_____

_____

_____

_____

_____

_____

_____

_____

_____

_____

_____

_____

_____

Guest Name
(address/phone #/email)

Notes

_____

_____

_____

_____

_____

_____

_____

_____

_____

_____

_____

_____

_____

Guest Name
(address/phone #/email)

Notes

_____

_____

_____

_____

Guest Name
(address/phone #/email)

Notes

Guest Name
(address/phone #/email)

Notes

_____

_____

_____

_____

_____

_____

_____

_____

_____

_____

_____

_____

_____

_____

Guest Name
(address/phone #/email)

Notes

Guest Name
(address/phone #/email)

Notes

Guest Name
(address/phone #/email)

Notes

Guest Name
(address/phone #/email)

Notes

Made in the USA
Lexington, KY
30 July 2019